Scott Foresman

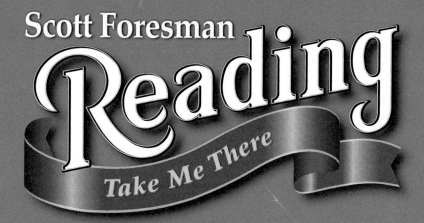

Scott Foresman
Reading
Take Me There

Good Times We Share

Take a Closer Look

Let's Learn Together

Favorite Things Old and New

Take Me There

Surprise Me!

PEARSON

Scott
Foresman

About the Cover Artist

Maryjane Begin and her family live in Providence, Rhode Island, where she teaches college students when she is not working on her own art. Many of her illustrations—even imaginary places—show how things in Providence look.

Cover illustration © Maryjane Begin

ISBN 0-328-03931-4

7 8 9 10 V063 10 09 08 07 06 05 04

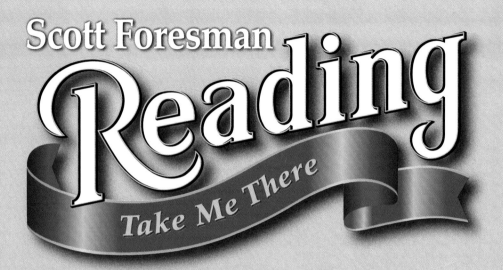

Scott Foresman
Reading
Take Me There

Program Authors

Peter Afflerbach

James Beers

Camille Blachowicz

Candy Dawson Boyd

Wendy Cheyney

Deborah Diffily

Dolores Gaunty-Porter

Connie Juel

Donald Leu

Jeanne Paratore

Sam Sebesta

Karen Kring Wixson

PEARSON

Scott Foresman

Editorial Offices: Glenview, Illinois • Parsippany, New Jersey • New York, New York
Sales Offices: Parsippany, New Jersey • Duluth, Georgia • Glenview, Illinois
Coppell, Texas • Ontario, California • Mesa, Arizona

Contents

4

Unit 5

SEE HOW THEY GROW
FOAL

DINOSAUR BABIES
By Lucille Recht Penner
Illustrated by Peter Barrett

LOST IN
THE MUSEUM
Story by Miriam Cohen
Pictures by Lillian Hoban

Unit 5

Where will we go?

How will we grow?

A Real Gift

by Diane Hoyt-Goldsmith

photos by Lawrence Migdale

This is Nayeli Lopez.

She reads with her cat. She gives him something to eat too.

Nayeli lives in the country.

She rides the bus to school.

It is loud, but Nayeli does not mind.

For Nayeli, loud sounds are soft.

It's hard for her to tell what people

are saying.

Nayeli can speak with her hands.
She knows how to make signs
for words.

One day, Nayeli had something to do. She met her mother right after school. "We can go now," her mother signed with her hands.

They stopped to buy a treat.

Nayeli picked out a peach to eat.

Then they passed a soccer team.

They stopped to watch the game.

Nayeli wanted to stay,

but she had something to do.

Nayeli saw a dog.

It wanted to play or be petted.

"No," signed her mother.

"I think we have to go now."

Nayeli walked very fast.

They had only one more block to go.

She didn't want to be late.

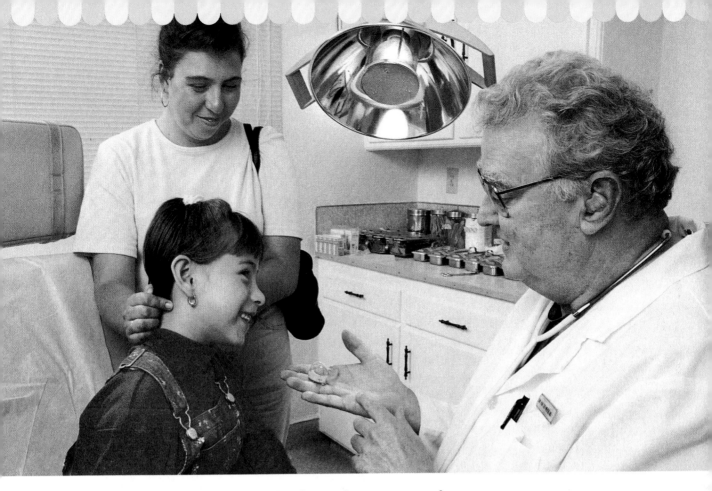

Now Nayeli had something to
help her. It fit just right.
The doctor's words sounded loud.

"Thank you" signed Nayeli
with her hands.

Arthur's Reading Race

by Marc Brown

Arthur learned to
read in school.

Now Arthur reads everywhere!
He reads in the car.

He reads in bed.

He reads
to his puppy, Pal.

Arthur even reads
to his little sister, D.W.

One day Arthur said,
"I can teach YOU to read too."

"I already know how to read,"
said D.W.

"You do not!" said Arthur.

"Do too!" said D.W.

"Prove it," said Arthur.
"Read ten words, D.W.,
   and I'll buy you an ice cream."

D.W. stuck out her hand.
"It's a deal," she said.
"Let's go!"

They raced to the park.
Arthur pointed to a sign.
"What's that say?" he asked.

"Zoo," said D.W.
"Easy as pie."

"I spy three words,"
said Arthur.

"Me too," said D.W.

"Taxi, gas, milk."

Arthur stepped off the curb.

"Look out!" said D.W.
"It says Don't Walk.
You could get hit by a car."

"All right,
Miss Smarty-Pants,
what's that say?"
asked Arthur.

"Police," said D.W.
"And you better
keep off the grass
or the police will get you."

"Bank," said D.W.
"I have a bank.

I hide my money in it
so you can't find it.
Bank makes eight words."

"We're almost home,"
   said Arthur.
"Too bad.
   You only read
   eight words.
   No ice cream
   for you today."

"Hold your horses," said D.W.
"I spy . . . ice cream.
  Hot dog! I read ten words.
  Let's eat!"

D.W. and Arthur ran
to the ice cream store.
Arthur bought two big cones.

Strawberry for D.W.
and chocolate for himself.
"Yummy," said D.W.

Arthur sat down.

"Sit down with me," said Arthur,

"and I'll read you my book."

"No," said D.W.

"I'll read YOU the book."

Arthur shook his head.
"I don't think so," he said.
"There are too many words
that you don't know."

D.W. laughed.
"Get up, Arthur."

"Now I can teach you
two words that you don't know,"
said D.W.
"WET PAINT!"

About the Author and Illustrator

Marc Brown

Arthur is a very famous aardvark! Arthur first appeared years ago. Marc Brown's son wanted to hear a bedtime story. Mr. Brown told one about an aardvark. Now there are more than thirty books about Arthur and D.W. You may have even seen Arthur on TV.

Reader Response

Let's Talk

Look back in the story. Find all the words D.W. reads in the pictures. What other words can you find?

Test Prep

Let's Write

Look around your room. What do you see that would be good for a game of "I Spy"? On a piece of paper write "I spy." Then write clues about what you see.

Let's Think

Do you think D.W. really can read? How might she know the words without reading them?

Today is Monday
It is sunny.
It is a gym day.

COLORS

BLUE
WHITE
BROWN

red

FOOD

APPLE
rice

ANIMALS

HORSE
PIG

CITIES

TAMPA
Chicago
NEW YORK

Go on a Word Hunt

Arthur and D.W. hunted for words.
You and a partner can too. Here's how:

1. Look in magazines and newspapers for
words you can sort. They might be words
for colors, foods, cities, names, and animals.

2. Cut out the words and mix them up.

3. Take turns picking a word and putting
it in the right pile.

Language Arts

Adjectives

An **adjective** is a word that tells more about a noun. A **noun** is a person, place, animal, or thing. An adjective can tell about size, color, and shape.

The children are in a **big** room.
The boy wears **blue** shorts.
Square books are by the plant.

The words in yellow are adjectives. What do the adjectives tell more about?

Talk

What nouns can you talk about in the picture? Use adjectives to tell more about them.

Write

Write the sentences. Draw a line
under each adjective.

1. **The green parrot talks.**
2. **The girl wears a striped sweater.**
3. **Toys are on low tables.**

Write your own sentences. Use an adjective
in each one. Draw a line under the adjectives.

A Big Day for Jay

by Lily Hong

It was noisy and crowded. Jay tugged at his dad. "When can we ride the Fire Dragon?" asked Jay. "I can't wait and I'm not afraid." His dad didn't hear him.

He tugged at his mom. "This isn't fun, Mom. All the jars look the same. Don't you want to see the Fire Dragon?"

All she said was, "Okay, we'll go soon."

They walked by
the animals.
   "Pig," said little Kate.
   "Cow," said Mother.
   "Sheep," said Father.
   "Fire Dragon!" yelled
Jay as he read the sign.

They walked from the tent to the Fire Dragon. People were everywhere. They were going this way and that. A girl with a big gray dog bumped into Jay.

"Mom, Dad," said Jay. No one called back. Jay knew where he was. But where was his family?

Then Jay spotted a police officer. He acted brave. "I'll be okay," he said. "I'll tell her my name and where I live."

"Let's go to the Lost and Found," said the police officer. "It's by the train. We can wait for your family there. Okay?"

"Did you get lost today too?" Jay asked the little pup at the Lost and Found.

Then the door opened. "Dog!" said Kate. "Jay!" said Mother. "Now let's find the Fire Dragon!" smiled Father.

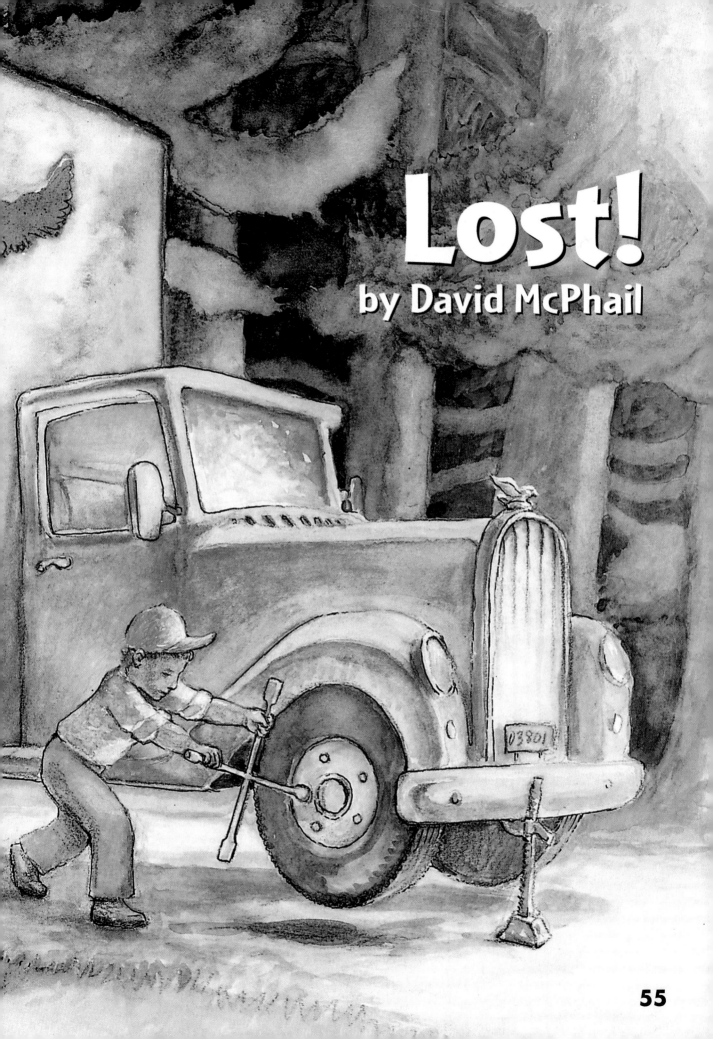

Lost!
by David McPhail

I am walking down the street
when I hear someone crying.

It's a bear!

He looks lost and afraid.

The tall buildings scare him.

And he's never seen so many people.

"Don't worry," I tell him.

"The buildings won't hurt you,
and most of the people are friendly."

"How did you get here?" I ask.

"I climbed in to have a nap," he explains, "and when I woke up, I was *lost!*"

"I'll help you. Tell me where you live."

"There are trees where I live,"

he tells me.

So we find some trees.

"More trees," he says, "and water!"

I take him to a place where there
are more trees—and water too.
"No," he says. "This is not it either."

I have an idea. "Follow me!" I say.

I take him to a tall building.

We go inside, get on the elevator,
and ride all the way to the top.

From up here we can see the
whole city. "Look!" I say.
"Now we can find your home."

"There it is!" he says, pointing.

Down we go, across three
streets and into the park.

The park is not the bear's home
after all—but he likes it there.

We go for a boat ride,

we have lunch,

and we go to the playground.

We are having a good time.

But it is getting late, and the

bear is still lost.

"Let's try the library," I tell him.

"We can find out anything here!"

Inside the library we look
through lots of books.
The bear sees a picture that
looks like his home.

We find the place on a map and hurry outside.

A bus is leaving.

We get on the bus and
ride for a long time.

Finally, we are there.

"*This* is where I live!" says
the bear.

He gives me a hug and
thanks me again for my help.
Then he waves good-bye and
disappears into the forest.

The trees are so tall, and
there aren't any people.
"Wait!" I call to the bear,
"come back!"

"I think I'm lost!" I tell him.

"Don't worry," he says.

"I will help you."

About the Author and Illustrator

David McPhail spends more time doing his artwork than he does writing his stories. When he gets an idea for a story, Mr. McPhail says, "It feels as if I'm about to win something." Do you feel that way about good ideas too?

Reader Response

Let's Talk

Would you help the bear? Why or why not?

Let's Think

How does the bear get lost? Why is the boy lost? Look back at the story and pictures.

Test Prep
Let's Write

Write a news story. Tell about the lost bear. Tell how the boy helps him.

Make a Map

Think about the way you go
to school from your home.
Make a map.

1. Draw your home at one end of
   the paper. Draw your school at the
   other end.
2. Draw a path from your home to your
   school. Use → → →.
3. Show some things you see along the
   way. Is there a park? Are there stores?
4. Share your map with your class.

Language Arts

Adjectives That Tell Color and Shape

Adjectives are words that describe. They tell more about nouns.

Red, yellow, and *blue* are adjectives that tell color.

The boy met a **brown** bear.

Round, square, and *lumpy* are adjectives that tell what shape something is.

They looked at a **round** globe.

Talk

What adjectives can you use to tell about the color and shape of things you see in the picture?

Write

Write the sentences. Draw a line under adjectives that tell about color and shape.

1. **The boy has a red hat.**
2. **The brown bear wants to go home.**
3. **The square box is full of newspapers.**

Write your own sentences. Use an adjective in each sentence to tell about color or shape. Draw a line under each adjective.

Baby Otter Grows Up

by Susan McCloskey
illustrated by Anna Vojtech

This is a baby otter. A baby otter is called a kit. This kit is three months old and still growing.

The kit rides on his mom's back. He is holding on to her coat to keep from slipping.

One day, his mom slips into the
water. This is something new!
The kit is afraid. But his mom does
not go back to the land. She keeps
swimming around in the water.

Soon the kit's mom comes out
of the water. Then she slides in
again. This time, her kit likes
sailing on her back. Mom is like
a small boat.

One day the kit's mom swims into deep water. The little kit is holding on to her back. He seems to like floating around.

Look! The kit's mom is sinking!
What will happen to the kit? Will
he sink or float?

The kit will float. He can swim!
But his mom had to show him that
he could.

Now the kit is almost grown. He swims well. He swims around the slow ducks. He can float on his back too.

Best of all, he can play in the
water with his friends.

FOAL

by Mary Ling
photos by Gordon Clayton

Newborn

I am a foal, a newborn pony. My legs are very wobbly.

My mother feeds me her warm milk as soon as I struggle to my feet.

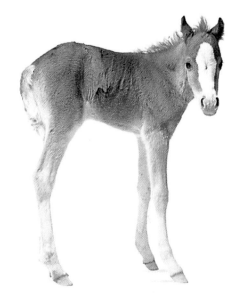

I feel stronger
after my milk.
I can stand up tall.

In the meadow

I am one week old.

I grow bigger every day.

I spend my days
in the meadow
with my mother.

I cuddle close
to her when the
wind blows.

I love feeling
the soft grass
beneath my
hooves.

Looking for Mommy

I am two weeks old.

I have two new teeth.

I want to show my mother.

Where is she?

I neigh loudly to her.

I hope she
hears me.

Soon my mother
comes. She is never
very far away.

Come and play

I am five weeks old.

Today will be a fun day!

A friend has come to play.

We play our
games and run
around the field.

When we are
tired, we graze
together.
The fresh grass
tastes sweet.

101

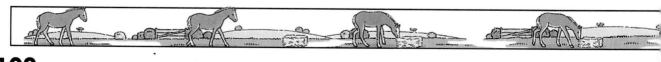

Crunchy apples

I am eight weeks old.

I gallop around the

fields every day.

Running and jumping

makes me very hungry.

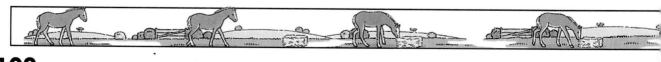

Look at these crunchy red apples. They smell yummy. I wonder if I can eat one?

Long legs

I am four months old.

My coat is chestnut brown now.

My long legs are sturdy.

I do not wobble anymore.

I am growing taller every day.

I am almost as tall as my mother.

In the field

I am five months old and
nearly full-grown.

Soon I will be
big enough to
join the other
ponies in the field.

See how I grew

Newborn

One week old

Two weeks old   Five weeks old   Eight weeks old

Four months old   Five months old

Everything Grows

by Raffi

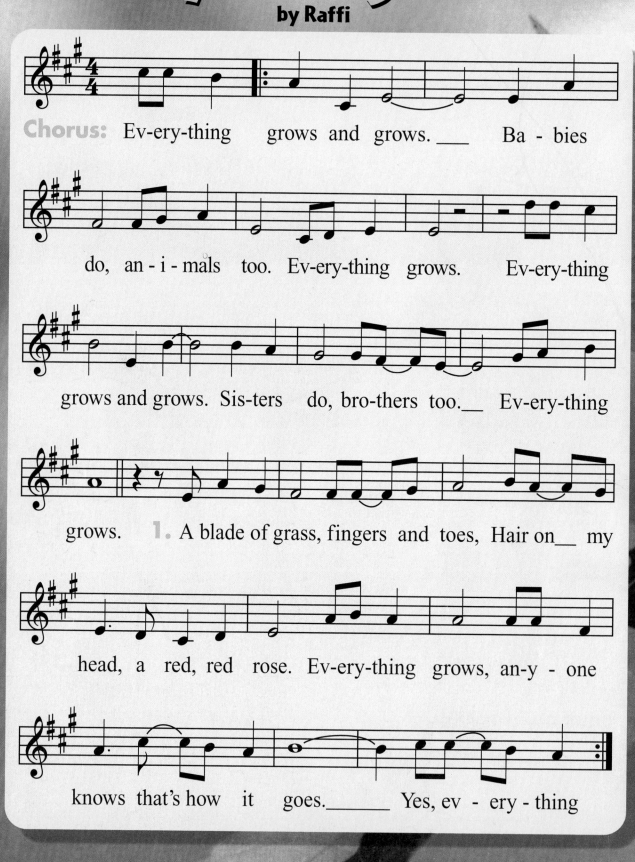

Chorus: Ev-ery-thing grows and grows.___ Ba - bies

do, an - i - mals too. Ev-ery-thing grows. Ev-ery-thing

grows and grows. Sis-ters do, bro-thers too.__ Ev-ery-thing

grows. **1.** A blade of grass, fingers and toes, Hair on__ my

head, a red, red rose. Ev-ery-thing grows, an-y - one

knows that's how it goes._____ Yes, ev - ery - thing

2. Food on the farm, fish in the sea,
   Birds in the air, leaves on the tree.
   Everything grows, anyone knows,
   That's how it goes.

3. That's how it goes, under the sun.
   That's how it goes, under the rain.
   Everything grows, anyone knows.
   That's how it goes.

Reader Response

Let's Talk

What things can a foal do that a newborn human baby can not?

Let's Think

The author writes facts about real horses but lets the foal tell the facts. Do you like this kind of writing? Tell why.

Test Prep

Let's Write

Write a report about another young animal. Let your animal tell the facts.

Tell what your animal is like as a baby. Tell what it is like when it grows up.

Make an Album

1. Bring in or draw a picture of yourself when you were little.

2. Under the picture write something you could do at that age.

3. Make more pictures. Tie your pictures into an album.

I could walk at 1.

Language Arts

Adjectives That Tell Size

Adjectives are words that describe nouns.

Some adjectives tell about the size of something. *Big, little, tall,* and *small* are some adjectives that tell size.

small mice   **big cat**

Talk

Look at the pictures. Make a list of adjectives that tell about size.

Write

Write the sentences. Draw a line under the adjectives.

1. Big cows stand in the barn.

2. A tall boy feeds the chickens.

3. A small puppy runs.

Write your own sentences. Use adjectives from your list. Draw a line under the adjectives.

What a Sight!

by Carolyn Crimi

illustrated by
Darryl Ligasan

Nicky and Jim were playing together
with Nicky's game.

"We're going to the museum!"
Dad said.

"Right now?" asked Jim.

"I'll tell Mom first," said Dad.

116

Nicky petted Tiger's fur and sighed. "I wish we could bring Tiger. He might like to go. But I guess museums are not for cats."

"I think you're right," said Jim.

Jim and Nicky got dressed to go to the museum. They didn't see Tiger sneak into Jim's backpack. Tiger hid right inside.

Dad, Nicky, and Jim walked down the museum's halls. They looked at the bright paintings hanging high on the walls. Tiger looked out of Jim's backpack.

They saw an apple pie and a lion
that liked to lie in the shade. Tiger
seemed to like the lion the best.

Then Tiger saw a painting of a very big dog. It made him start to move around. He jumped out of Jim's backpack!

"Tiger!" Nicky called. "Is that you?"

Together, Nicky and Jim ran after Tiger. He gave one man a fright. Soon everyone ran after Tiger. What a sight! Jim found him at last.

Dad's face was red from running. "Tiger, it isn't right to sneak into a museum," he said.

"You've been a bad kitty," said Jim. "But I bet you had fun!"

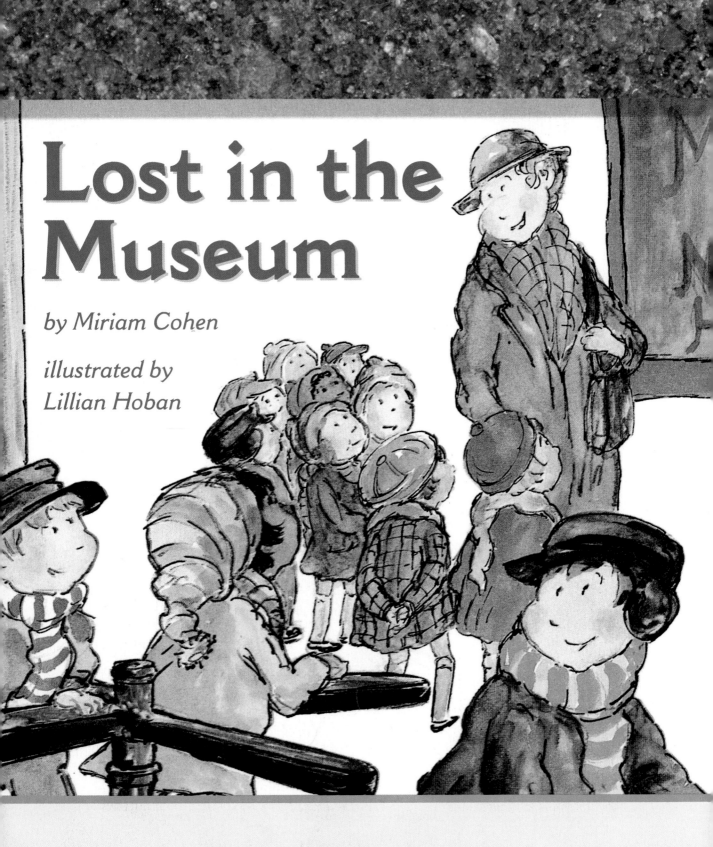

Lost in the Museum

by *Miriam Cohen*

illustrated by
Lillian Hoban

"This is a big place,"
the teacher told the first grade.

"But if we all stay together,
nobody will get lost in the museum."

Danny said to Jim,
"I know where the dinosaur is.
Come on, I'll show you!"

Jim had never seen a dinosaur.
He ran after Danny.
And Willy and Sammy,
Paul, and George did too.

Anna Maria and Sara started after them.
"Come back! You'll get lost!" they called.

Danny slid down the hall very fast.
He slid into a room at the end.
Willy and Sammy, Paul, George, Jim,
Anna Maria, and Sara ran after him.

But Jim stopped.
He put his head way back.
He looked up.

Jim heard Willy say,
"That is some big chicken!"

"It's the dinosaur!" shouted Danny.

Jim came around the corner.
The dinosaur had his arms up over
Jim's head. The dinosaur's teeth
were smiling a fierce smile.

Paul said, "Look out, Jim!
He's going to get you!"

Jim turned and ran as fast as he could.
"Jim, stop! I was only fooling," Paul called.

The kids came running after Jim.
"Don't worry. He won't hurt you," said Sammy.

"That's right," Willy told Jim.
"They don't have dinosaurs anymore."

Paul put his arm around Jim.

Anna Maria said, "It's silly to be scared."

Jim knew it was silly.

He wished he could be brave.

"Come on, let's find the others," George said.

"I think we are lost," said Sara.

"I know where to go," Danny said.

They all hurried after him down the big
hall. But there were too many rooms.

"You got us lost," Anna Maria said
to Danny.

"My toe hurts," said George.

"Maybe we will have to stay here
all night," Paul said.

Jim thought about staying all night
with the dinosaur.
"I will go find the teacher," he said.
"You stay here in case she comes."

Jim went into many rooms. He kept
his eyes shut a little. If he saw the
dinosaur, he could shut them tight.

A big boy was looking at birds' eggs.
Jim said, "Have you seen my teacher?"
Before the big boy could answer,
Jim saw a red coat way down the hall.

Margaret had a red coat! Jim ran to see.
But somebody else was wearing
Margaret's coat!

Jim was so tired.
He had to find the teacher!
He had to bring her back to the kids!
He ran on.

Jim saw penguins playing in the snow like first graders. He saw a mother, father, and a child deer. The father stood with one foot in the air.

Jim stopped to rest.
The room was dark.
At first he couldn't see.

Then a great gray whale swam over
his head. He winked at Jim as if
he had something nice to tell him.
Jim looked all the way to the whale's tail.

A lady was there with many children.
"Jim!" everybody called. "Oh, Jim!
We have been looking for you!"

The teacher said, "Where have you been?
Where are the other children?"

"I'll take you there," Jim said.

Jim started back.
He went past the penguins, past the deer.
This way? No! That way!
There they were—George, Willy and Sammy,
Anna Maria, Danny, Paul, and Sara.

When they saw their teacher,
George and Sara began to cry.
She hugged them.
"If we had stayed together, this
wouldn't have happened," she said.

Willy and Sammy said, "Jim was brave.
He went to find you!"

"Yes," the teacher said, "Jim was very brave.
But next time, remember—IF WE ALL STAY
TOGETHER, NOBODY WILL GET LOST."

They were so glad to be found!
Everybody went to have lunch in the cafeteria.
You could choose chicken and dumplings,
crisp fried fish, or beef stew with two vegetables.
But they all chose hot dogs.

Museum Map

Here is a map of the museum the first grade visited. Some children got lost. This map might have helped them. It shows the rooms in the museum.

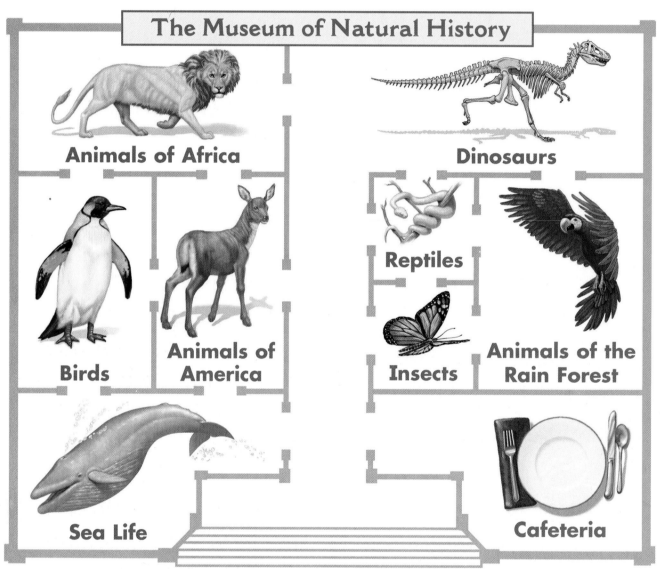

The Museum of Natural History

Animals of Africa

Dinosaurs

Birds

Animals of America

Reptiles

Insects

Animals of the Rain Forest

Sea Life

Cafeteria

Let's Talk

Where did Jim find his teacher?
What could you see in this museum?

About the Author and the Illustrator

Author

Miriam Cohen

Miriam Cohen wrote eighteen books about Jim and the other first graders. Ms. Cohen says that Jim is based on her three sons. She says Jim is a "rolling and patting together of Adam, Gabe, and Jem into one little guy."

Illustrator

Lillian Hoban

Do you like to visit museums? Lillian Hoban did when she was your age. Those visits may have given her ideas for the pictures in *Lost in the Museum.*

Ms. Hoban also loved to draw and read as a child. Now she draws the pictures for all of Miriam Cohen's books.

Reader Response

Let's Talk

What would you want to see in a museum? What would you do if you got lost?

Let's Think

Does Jim think that the museum in the story is fun or scary or both? Why?

Test Prep

Let's Write

Jim and his class went to a museum. Tell about a place you would like to go with your class. Tell why you want to go there.

Readers Theater

Read and act out the story as a play.

1. One person reads what the teacher says.
2. Choose who will read the parts of Jim, Anna Maria, Sara, Danny, Paul, Willy, Sammy, and George.
3. Choose other children to play the rest of the first-grade class.

Language Arts

Adjectives That Tell What Kind

Adjectives are words that describe nouns.

Some adjectives tell what kind. *Happy, sad, funny,* and *scary* are adjectives you can use to tell what kind.

Lost in the Museum is a **scary** story.

Talk

What kinds of books do you see in the picture? Make a list of adjectives that tell what kind.

TRUE BOOKS

SCARY BOOKS

I MISS MY DOG

SAD BOOKS

Book Fair

Write

Write the sentences. Draw
a line under the adjectives that tell what kind.

1. *Glasses for D.W.* has a **happy** ending.
2. *Mama and Papa Have a Store* tells
   a **true** story.
3. *John Willy and Freddy McGee* is a
   funny story.

Write your own sentence about a book you like.
Use an adjective that tells what kind of book it is.
Draw a line under the adjective.

Chompy's Afternoon
by G. Brian Karas

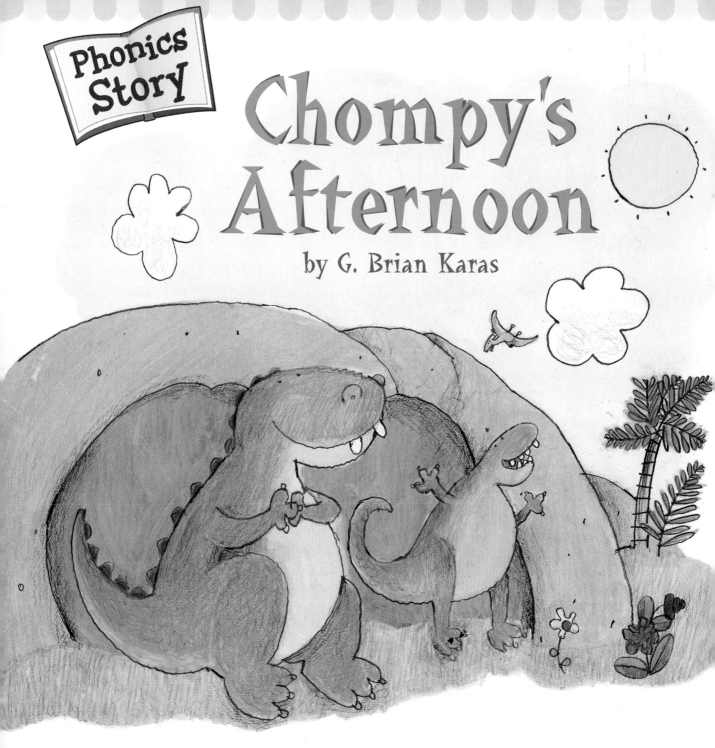

Chompy looked up at the blue sky.
"It's a nice afternoon," he said.
   "Let's have a picnic," said Mom.
   "I'm so happy!" said Chompy.
Chompy loved picnics more than
anything.

Chompy packed yummy food. He packed everything he could find. "I'll even pack these huge watermelons," he said.

Chompy was very hungry.

"My, my, Chompy. This is too much food," said Mom.

"I'll try to carry it," said Chompy. Chompy couldn't carry it all.

So Mom put most of the food back. Then she packed two cupcakes.

Chompy and his mom walked up
the pathway to a hilltop. They sat
down by a waterfall.
"It's very pretty here," said Mom.
They ate most of their food.

"I'm still hungry. I think I'll take a little walk," Chompy thought. Chompy looked around for more food.

"There has to be something to eat somewhere!" he thought.

"I'm so lucky," said Chompy.
"Here is a nice little treat." He took a
big bite.

But it was not nice or little or a
treat. It was a huge, mean animal.

Chompy heard a big roar.
"I'm not so lucky!" yelled Chompy.
He ran as fast as he could.
Mom heard Chompy cry. "Go
away, you big bully!" she roared.

The animal ran far away. Chompy
and his mom went back to the
hilltop.

"Here is a little treat, Chompy,"
said Mom. "And it won't bite back."
Chompy was very happy now.

Dinosaur Babies

by Lucille Recht Penner
illustrated by Peter Barrett

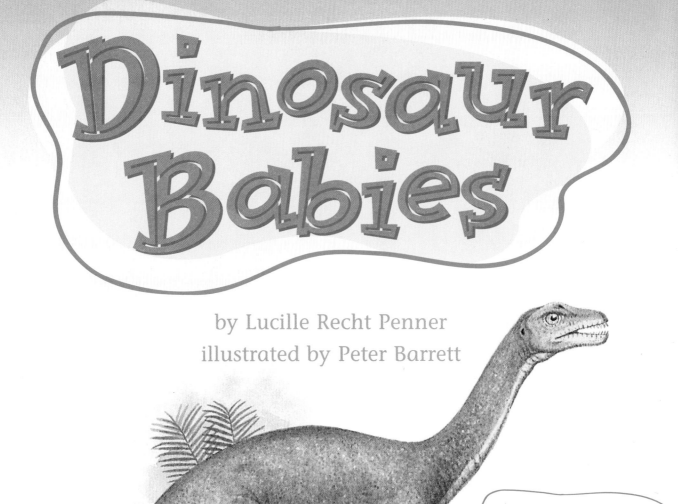

Apatosaurus
(a–PAT–uh–sor–us)

Squeak! Squeak!

Is that the sound of a baby

dinosaur calling to its mother?

Nobody knows.

Nobody has ever heard
a baby dinosaur.

Nobody has seen one.

All the dinosaurs died millions of years ago. But we know a lot about them from what dinosaur hunters have found . . .

footprints

teeth

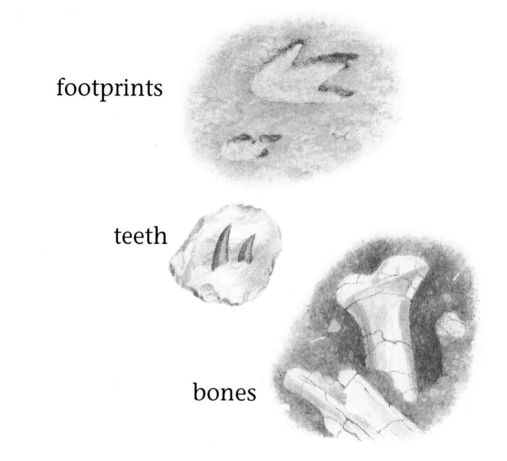

bones

They have found small baby bones in nests.

They have even found dinosaur eggs.

Most dinosaurs were very big.

But their eggs were small.

The smallest was only as big as a quarter.

The biggest was about the size
of a football!

Were dinosaurs good mothers?

This kind of dinosaur was.

She made a nest of mud and

laid her eggs in it.

Chickens sit on their eggs.

But this dinosaur did not.

She was too heavy.

The eggs would break!

She put leaves on the eggs

to keep them warm.

Maiasaura
(my–uh–SOR–uh)

The mother watched the nest.

Lots of animals liked to eat dinosaur eggs!

She kept them away.

Inside the eggs the babies grew.
They breathed through tiny holes
in the eggshells.

Troödon
(TRO–o–don)

One day the eggs
cracked!
Little baby dinosaurs
came out.
They were hungry.
Maybe they squeaked.

The mother dinosaur
brought them food.
The babies ate and ate
all day long.

Dinosaur babies had big heads and big eyes.

They could see and hear well.

Human babies are born without any teeth.

Not dinosaur babies! They had lots of teeth.

Tyrannosaurus
(tie–RAN–uh–SOR–us)

Apatosaurus
(a–PAT–uh–sor–us)

What did baby dinosaurs eat?
Some kinds ate leaves and
berries and seeds.

Some kinds ate little animals
and bugs.

Deinonychus
(die–NON–ee–kus)

Was it safe for baby dinosaurs

to hunt for food alone? No!

Enemies were all around.

And baby dinosaurs could not

fight or run fast.

They could only hide.

Psittacosaurus
(SIT–uh–ko–SOR–us)

Tyrannosaurus
(tie–RAN–uh–SOR–us)

177

Some baby dinosaurs were lucky.

They were never alone.

They lived in herds.

Even then enemies tried to grab
the babies and eat them!

So the dinosaurs made a circle.

Little ones stayed on the inside.

Big ones guarded the outside.

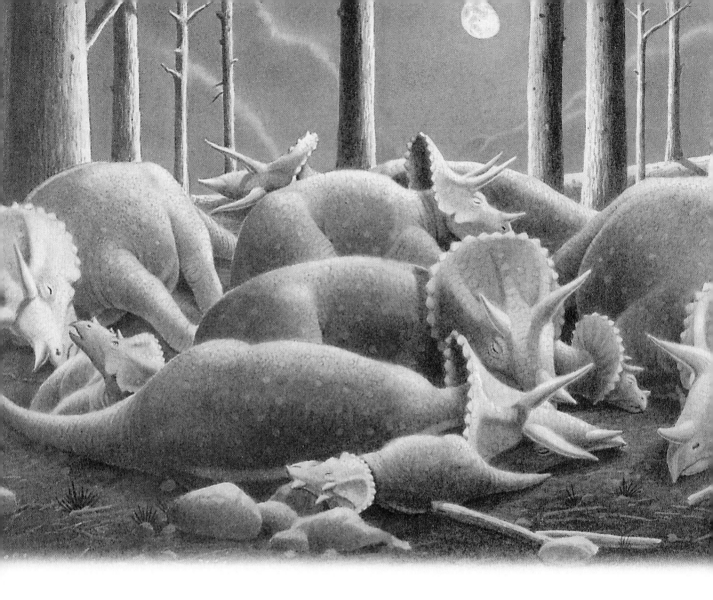

Babies were safe in the
dinosaur herd.
The dinosaurs walked and
ate and slept together.

Baby dinosaurs kept growing and changing.

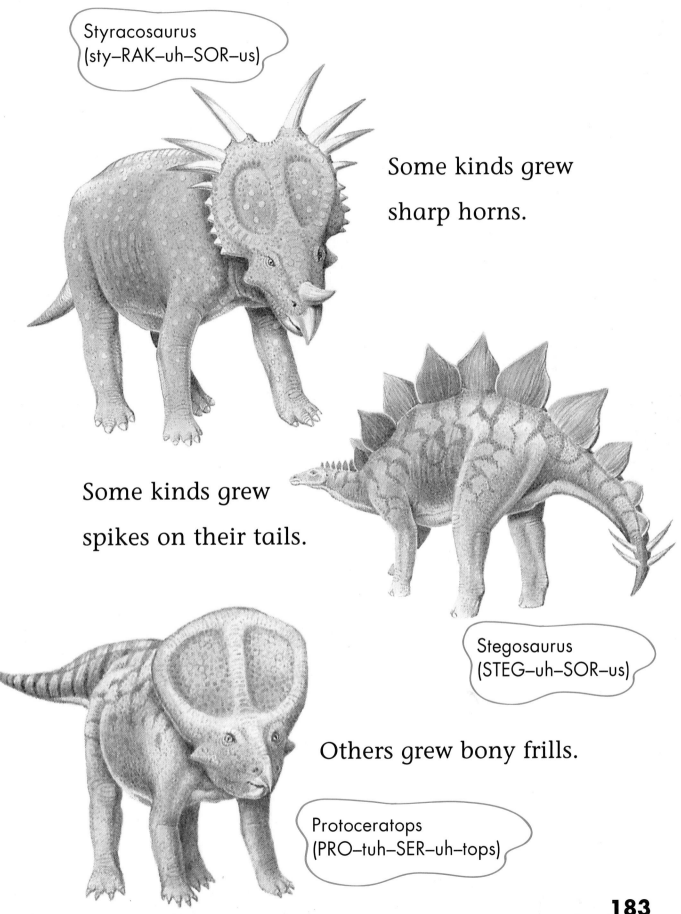

Styracosaurus
(sty–RAK–uh–SOR–us)

Some kinds grew
sharp horns.

Some kinds grew
spikes on their tails.

Stegosaurus
(STEG–uh–SOR–us)

Others grew bony frills.

Protoceratops
(PRO–tuh–SER–uh–tops)

They grew until they weren't
babies anymore.
Some grew to be the biggest
animals ever to walk the Earth!
And some had dinosaur babies
of their own.

Something Big Has Been Here

by Jack Prelutsky

Something big has been here,
what it was, I do not know,
for I did not see it coming,
and I did not see it go,
but I hope I never meet it,
if I do, I'm in a fix,
for it left behind its footprints,
they are size nine-fifty-six.

Unfortunately

by Bobbi Katz

Dinosaurs lived so long ago

they never had a chance to know

how many kids would love to get

a dinosaur to be their pet!

Reader Response

Let's Talk

What did you learn about dinosaurs?
What surprised you?

Let's Think

Look back at the stories "Foal"
and "Dinosaur Babies." How is
a baby dinosaur different from
a foal? How are they the same?

Test Prep

Let's Write

Pretend that you lived in the days
of the dinosaurs. Write sentences.
Tell what would you have liked most
about it. Tell what would you have
liked least about it.

Make a Dinosaur

You know a lot about how dinosaurs lived and how they looked. You can make a dinosaur of your own.

1. Get what you need.
2. Shape a dinosaur out of clay.
3. Make a home for your dinosaur. Put it inside.
4. Write the dinosaur's name on the top of the box.

Language Arts

Adjectives That Tell How Many

Words for numbers can be **adjectives**. These adjectives tell how many.

This dinosaur has **three** horns.
There are **ten** eggs in the nest.

Talk

Look at the pictures. Tell what you see. What adjectives will you use to tell how many?

Write

Write the sentences. Circle the adjectives
that tell how many.

1. **Some footprints show four toes.**
2. **One nest has ten eggs in it.**
3. **Tyrannosaurus ran on two legs.**

Write your own sentences.
Use adjectives that tell how many.
Circle the adjectives.

The True Story of Abbie Burgess

by Fay Robinson
illustrated by Lane DuPont

Abbie Burgess watches her dad
leave. While he is away, she'll do
his job.

She'll light the lamps in the lighthouse. The lamps help people in boats see the rocks better.

Abbie looks out at the sea. She puts out her hand. She feels a few raindrops. The wind blows branches into the blue water and tosses the boats around. A big storm is on its way!

Abbie knows she must light the lamps right away. She dashes up the steps. Rain washes over the lighthouse.

Abbie lights the lamps one by one. Now boat crews can see the rocks, and they can keep their boats away. Abbie watches as a boat passes by safely.

All night, Abbie rushes up
the steps to check the lights.
They must stay lit. She doesn't
sleep at all. She won't give up.
At last, the night is over.
Abbie's dad will be back soon.

But her dad can't come back because it is still raining!

Night after night, Abbie lights the lamps. Again and again, boats go around the rocks safely.

At last, the storm is over. Abbie's dad comes back. He gives Abbie a hug. He knew she could do the job!

Abbie Burgess helped a lot of people. She was a true hero.

The Bravest Cat!

The True Story of Scarlett

by Laura Driscoll

illustrated by Fred Willingham

Brooklyn, NY, 1996

A building is on fire!

There are lots of fire engines and
lots of firefighters.

It is a big fire in an old garage.

But one thing is lucky.

No one lives in the building.

Wait! Look!

What do the firefighters see?

It is a cat!

She runs out of the garage.

She is carrying something—

something small.

It is a tiny kitten!

The cat puts her kitten
in a safe place.
Then she runs back into the fire!
What is she doing?

Soon the cat runs out again—
with another kitten!

She runs in and out

three more times.

The firefighters cannot believe their eyes.

Now there is a pile of kittens!

They are tiny and scared.

One has burns on his little ears.

And the poor mother cat!

Her burns are bad.

Her eyes are hurt.

She cannot even see her kittens.

So she touches each kitten with

her nose.

One, two, three, four, five.

They are all there.

Very gently, a firefighter puts
all of the cats into a box.
He can tell they need a doctor.
The firefighter takes the cats
to the animal hospital.

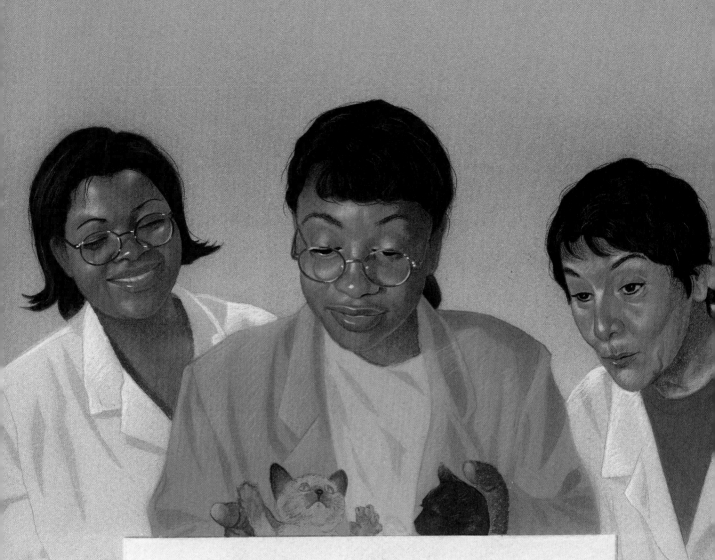

The cats do not belong to anyone.
They are strays. So the doctors
give the mother cat a name.
They call her Scarlett because of
her red burns.

Soon lots of people
know about Scarlett.
Newspapers run stories.
People want her to be on TV.
She is a hero and a star.

Brave Cat
Saves Kittens

Everyone hopes Scarlett will get better.
And slowly she does.
The kittens are kept in another room
so she can rest.
Scarlett cannot take care of
them anymore.

The people at the hospital
give the kittens lots of love.
And they get better too—
all except one.
The doctors think he was the last
kitten to get out of the fire.
The smoke hurt his lungs.
A month later, he dies.

But the other kittens get new homes.

And what about Scarlett?

Letters for her come from all
over the world.

So many people want to give her
a good home.

The people at the hospital
read more than 1,000 letters!
They try to find the best home
for Scarlett.

At last, they make up their minds.
TV and newspaper reporters
come to hear the big news.
A woman named Karen Wellen
will care for Scarlett.

In her letter, Karen wrote
about her own accident—
a car accident.
Like Scarlett, it took a long time
for Karen to get better.
She knows what Scarlett
has been through.

Karen also had a cat before.

She loved it a lot.

But Karen's cat died just after
her accident.

Karen did not want to get another cat—
unless it was a very special one . . .

just like Scarlett!

About the Illustrator

Fred Willingham

To make his drawings look real, Fred Willingham looks at photographs as he draws. Sometimes he takes the photographs. He uses his children and his friends as models. He used photos of cats in many poses when he drew the pictures for *The Bravest Cat!* He found those photos at the library. He knew just how to draw Scarlett because he saw a photograph of her.

...ttens
...ohn Livingston

Our cat had kittens
weeks ago
when everything outside was snow.

So she stayed in
and kept them warm
and safe from all the clouds and storm.

But yesterday
when there was sun
she snuzzled on the smallest one

and turned it over
from beneath
and took its fur between her teeth

and carried it
outside to see
how nice a winter day can be

and then our dog
decided he
would help her take the other three

and one by one
they took them out
to see what sun is all about

so when they're grown
they'll always know
to never be afraid of snow.

Read Together
Reader Response

Let's Talk

Scarlett is a hero.
Who else in the story
might be called a
hero? Why?

Let's Think

"The Bravest Cat" is a true story.
How do you know? Look back
in the story for clues.

Test Prep
Let's Write

Pretend that you are Scarlett.
Write in your journal about the
day of the fire. What do
you see, hear, and smell?

Make a Hero Award

Would you like to make an award for
a hero?

1. Draw a picture of your hero.
2. Make an award ribbon.
3. Write the name of your
hero on the ribbon.
4. Glue the ribbon to
your picture.

Language Arts

Adjectives Make Sentences Better

An **adjective** tells more about a person, place, animal, or thing. Adjectives make sentences better.

My dad has a **special** dog.
Drew has **black** fur and a **long** tail.
He helps Dad cross **busy** streets.
Drew is Dad's **good** friend.

Talk

Tell about the pictures. What adjectives do you use to tell about what you see? Tell how the adjectives make your sentences better.

Write

Write the sentences. Circle the adjectives.

1. The fluffy cat has white feet.

2. The happy baby looks out of the blue buggy.

3. The black dog helps the man.

Write your own sentences. Use adjectives. Tell how the adjectives make your sentences better.

A Real Gift

Arthur's Reading Race

buy   right
only   think
or

A Big Day for Jay

Lost!

don't   live
from   when
hear

Baby Otter Grows Up

FOAL

around   old
her   show
new

What a Sight!

Lost in the Museum

been   start
first   together
found

Chompy's Afternoon

animals   most
even   their
heard

The True Story of Abbie Burgess

The Bravest Cat!

because   give
better   people
burns   put

Choose the Right Answer

A test question may have three answer choices. Only one answer is right. How will you choose the right answer?

A test about *The Bravest Cat* might have this question.

1. **Who gave Scarlett a new home after the fire?**

Ⓐ **a woman who wanted a special cat**

Ⓑ **a doctor at the hospital**

Ⓒ **a fire engine**

Read the question. Find the important word. Think about each answer choice. Which choice is right?

Here is how one girl chose her answer.

The important word in the question is *Who*. It tells me the answer is a person. A fire engine is not a person. A doctor is a person, but a doctor did not take Scarlett. The answer is A.

Try it!

Use what you have learned to choose the right answer to this test question.

2. Where was the fire that hurt Scarlett?

Ⓐ **a firetruck**

Ⓑ **in a garage**

Ⓒ **in a house**

Glossary

Words from Your Stories

Aa

accident An **accident** is something bad that happens. We were in a car **accident**.

across He rode the bicycle **across** the tightrope.

across

almost I **almost** missed the bus. It is **almost** ten o'clock.

Bb

baby A **baby** is a very young child or animal. A **baby** cat is called a kitten.

believe When you **believe** something, you think it is true.

beneath **Beneath** means below or under. The dog's bone is **beneath** the bed.

beneath

bought He **bought** a new pair of shoes.

break If you **break** something, it comes apart or goes to pieces.

breathed If you **breathed**, you took in air through your nose or mouth.

buildings   Buildings have walls and a roof. Schools and houses are **buildings**.

building

burns   **Burns** are sores caused by too much heat. He got **burns** from the hot pan.

Cc

cafeteria   A **cafeteria** is a place to eat in a school or other building. You choose your food and carry it to a table.

climbed   If you **climbed**, you went up something. The squirrels **climbed** the post.

could   Her brother said she **could** come. She **could** run very fast.

crowded   **Crowded** means too full. The bus was very **crowded** this morning.

climbed

crowded

crying   If you are **crying**, you have tears coming from your eyes.

curb   A **curb** is the raised edge between the sidewalk and street.

233

Dd

dinosaur   A **dinosaur** is an animal that lived many years ago. **Dinosaurs** lived on Earth before there were people.

disappears   When something **disappears**, it goes out of sight.

Ee

Earth   **Earth** is the planet we live on.

eight   **Eight** is one more than seven, 8. Can you count **eight** cats?

else   Will someone **else** go in my place? Let's go somewhere **else** for lunch.

enemies   Your **enemies** are people or animals that wish to harm you.

eight

except   The store is open every day **except** Sunday.

Ff

field   A **field** is a piece of land without trees. The cows grazed in the **field**.

field

fierce   **Fierce** means very strong or dangerous.

fooling   If you are **fooling**, you are joking, teasing, or pretending.

found   She **found** a hat in the hall. She took it to the Lost and **Found**.

fur   **Fur** is hair that is thick and soft. **Fur** covers the skin of many animals.

Gg

garage   A **garage** is a place where cars are parked.

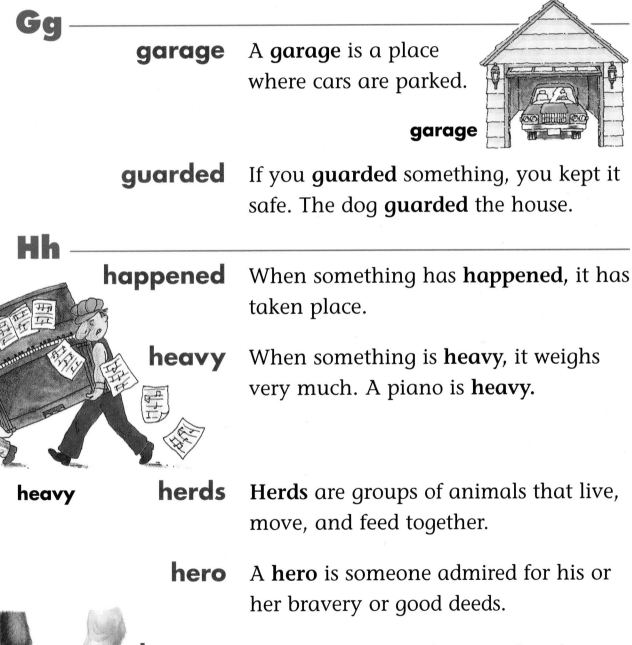

garage

guarded   If you **guarded** something, you kept it safe. The dog **guarded** the house.

Hh

happened   When something has **happened**, it has taken place.

heavy   When something is **heavy**, it weighs very much. A piano is **heavy**.

heavy

herds   **Herds** are groups of animals that live, move, and feed together.

hero   A **hero** is someone admired for his or her bravery or good deeds.

hooves   **Hooves** are more than one **hoof**. Horses, cows, and pigs have **hooves**.

hooves

235

hospital   A **hospital** is a place where sick people are cared for.

human   A **human** body is the body of a person.

hunters   **Hunters** are people who kill wild birds or animals for food or for sport.

hurried   If you **hurried**, you went very quickly. He **hurried** to catch the school bus.

hurried

hurt   If you **hurt** something or someone, you cause it pain.

Kk

knew   I **knew** her name. He **knew** the answer.

Ll

library   A **library** is a room or building where books are kept. You can take books out at most **libraries**.

library

Mm

millions   **Millions** means more than one million. A **million** is one thousand thousand, or 1,000,000.

minds   When people make up their **minds**, they decide about something.

months   **Months** are parts of a year. There are twelve **months** in a year.

months

museum   A **museum** is a building for keeping and showing interesting things.

Nn

neigh   To **neigh** is to make the sound that a horse makes.

newborn **Newborn** means only just born.

noisy   **Noisy** means full of noise. It is very **noisy** near the airport.

Oo

opened   When something has been **opened**, people and things can get in or out of it. The cat **opened** the drawer.

opened

otter   An **otter** is an animal with thick brown fur and strong claws.

Pp

paint   **Paint** is a liquid used to color things. **Paint** comes in many different colors.

penguins   **Penguins** are sea birds that dive and swim but do not fly. **Penguins** live in very cold places.

penguins

people   Men, women, and children are **people**.

ponies   **Ponies** are small horses.

prove   To **prove** something is to show that it is true.

Rr

reporters   **Reporter**s are people who write or tell news for a newspaper, magazine, or a radio or TV station.

roar   A **roar** is a loud, deep sound. The lion's **roar** frightened us.

Ss

safely   **Safely** means without harm or danger.

scared   **Scared** means afraid.

shook   If you **shook** your head, you moved it from side to side. It is a way to say no.

signs

signs   **Signs** are marks or words used to tell you something. Cars stop at stop **signs**.

soft Soft means not loud.

special Something that is **special** is unusual or different.

spy When you **spy** something, you see it and notice it. Meg **spies** footprints.

spy

stronger If you feel **stronger**, you have more power and health than before.

struggle To **struggle** is to work at something that is hard to do. Each team **struggled** to win.

struggle

Tt

thought If you had an idea about something, then you **thought** about it.

through The bird flew **through** the house. Are you **through** with your dinner?

Ww

wobbly **Wobbly** means shaky.

worry To **worry** is to feel upset and afraid.

Writer's Handbook

Contents

Sentences

A **sentence** is a group of words that tells a complete idea.
A sentence begins with a capital letter. Many sentences end with a **.**.
The pie is too hot to eat **.**

A **telling sentence** tells something.
It begins with a capital letter.
It ends with a **.**.
The girl lost her ring **.**

A **question** asks something.
A question is an asking sentence.
It begins with a capital letter.
It ends with a **?**.
Does Jill live on a farm?

An **exclamation** is a sentence that shows strong feelings.
An exclamation begins with a capital letter.
It ends with an **!**.
We can't wait to go to the circus!

A **command** is a sentence that tells someone to do something.
A command begins with a capital letter. It ends with a ..

Write your name on your paper.

Naming Parts

Every sentence has two parts.
It has a naming part and an action part.
The **naming part** names a person, animal, or thing.

The bird flies from the nest.

Action Parts

The **action part** of a sentence tells what a person, animal, or thing does.

The dog **chews on the bone.**

Word Order

The order of words tells what a sentence means.

The hat is on the cat.
The cat is on the hat.

Nouns

A **noun** is a word that names a person, place, animal, or thing.

The **apple** is red and juicy.

Nouns for One and More than One

Sometimes –**s** is added to the end of a noun.
An –**s** makes a noun mean more than one.

Firefighters help keep us safe.

Sometimes –**es** is added to the end of a noun.
Add –**es** to nouns that end in **x**, **s**, **ch**, or **sh**.

Put the **boxes** on the porch.
The **benches** are in the sun.

Writing with Nouns

A noun can be in the naming part of a sentence.
A noun can be in the action part of a sentence.

naming part	action part
The **girl** Mary	cooked our **dinner.**

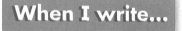

When I write...

I use nouns to give information.

Verbs

A **verb** tells what a person, animal, or thing does. Many verbs are action words.

Mom **swims** on a team.

Verbs for One

Verbs tell what one person, animal, or thing does. Add **–s** to these verbs.

Dad **sings** to me.

Verbs for Two or More

Verbs may tell what two or more people, animals, or things do. Do not add **–s** to these verbs.

The boy and girl **skip** rope.

Verbs for Now and for the Past

Verbs can tell about action that takes place now.

Dad and I **wash** the car.

Verbs can tell about action that happened in the past. Add **–ed** to the verb.

Yesterday, I **helped** my mom.

When I write...

I use verbs to tell what is happening.

Is, Are, Was, Were

Use **is** and **are** to tell about now.

The sky **is** blue.
The clouds **are** white.

Use **was** and **were** to tell about the past.

Tom **was** tired.
We **were** busy all day.

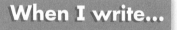

When I write...

I use verbs to tell *when* an action takes place.

Using the Word *Not*

The word **not** changes what a sentence means.
A verb and the word **not** can be put together. They make a shorter word called a **contraction**. The letter **o** is left out. An **'** is used in place of the letter **o.**

The fish **are not** hungry.
The fish **aren't** hungry.

Adjectives

An adjective is a word that tells more about a noun.
The **funny** clown led the parade.

An adjective can tell about color.

The **blue** room is my favorite.

An adjective can tell about shape.

The baby liked the **round** ball.

An adjective can tell about size.

Did you see the **big** tiger?

An adjective can tell what kind.

The **shiny** key fits the door.

An adjective can tell how many.

My sister has **twenty** marbles.

Pronouns

A pronoun is a word that can take the place of a noun.
These words are pronouns.

I	you	he	she	it
we	you	they		

Pronouns can be used in the naming part of a sentence.
They are:

I	he	she	we	they

Tomás is in my class.
He is in my class.

Pronouns can be used in the action part of a sentence.
They are:

me	him	her	us	them

Lindy read to **the children.**
Lindy read to **us.**

When I write...

I may use a noun in one sentence and a pronoun in the next. This makes my writing more interesting.

Capital Letters

People and pets have special names.
Special names begin with capital
letters. The word *I* is always a
capital letter.

My best friend is **Alex.**
I named my dog **Trooper.**

A title can come before the
name of a person.
A title begins with a capital letter.
Some titles end with a **.**.

Our neighbor is **Ms.** **Jane Kennedy.**
Do you know **Judge Andy Smith?**

The names of days, months,
and holidays begin with capital letters.

The **Fourth of July** is on a **Friday**
this year.

Writing a Letter

Most letters have five parts.
They are the **date, greeting, body, closing,** and **signature.**
A **comma** , goes between the date and year.
A comma is also used after the greeting and closing.

- Read this friendly letter.
- Look for the five parts.
- Look for three commas.

Date	May 3, 200_
Greeting	Dear Bill,
Body	How are you? I hope you are better. I was sorry to hear that you broke your leg. I guess a lot of people trip over their cats. I hope you are getting around all right. See you soon!
Closing	Your friend,
Signature	Ellen

Addressing an Envelope

Addressing an Envelope

After you write a letter, you can mail it.
Put the letter in an envelope.
Then seal the envelope.
Write your name and address in the
top left corner.
This is the **return address.**

Write the name and address of the
person you wrote to in the center of the
envelope. This is the **mailing address.**

Remember to put a stamp on your envelope.
Then it will be ready to mail.

Return address

Ellen Lee
2610 Union St.
Glenview, IL 60025

Mailing address

Bill Robins
2333 Sky Drive
Atlanta, GA 30301

Sharing a Book

Writing a book report is one way to
share a book.
Here is what you should
tell in your report.

- Title
- Author
- A little bit about the story
- One important thing that happens
  in the story
- Why you like the book – or don't
  like it

Here are some other ways to share a book.

- **Make a Book Cover**
  Draw a picture of a part you liked.
  Write the title and author of the book
  on your picture.

- **Be a Reporter**
  Be a radio or TV reporter.
  Tell about a favorite book.
  Tell why you liked it.

- **Act Out Your Book**
  Make stick puppets of characters
  in your book.
  With some friends, act out part of your book.

Spelling Lists

A Real Gift
Arthur's Reading Race

1.	**ask**	May I **ask** a question?
2.	**call**	Mom got a **call** from Dad.
3.	**clean**	Please **clean** your room.
4.	**asked**	I **asked** for a drink.
5.	**called**	Dad **called** the doctor.
6.	**cleaned**	I **cleaned** up the mess.
7.	**teach**	Please **teach** me to skate.
8.	**neat**	Dad looked **neat** in his suit.
9.	**think**	I **think** with my mind.
10.	**only**	There is **only** one cookie left.

A Big Day for Jay
Lost!

1.	**say**	I cannot **say** that word.
2.	**play**	Will you **play** a game with me?
3.	**may**	I **may** come to your party.
4.	**way**	Which **way** should I go?
5.	**wait**	I can't **wait** until tomorrow.
6.	**rain**	The **rain** wet my bike.
7.	**don't**	I **don't** know your name.
8.	**I'm**	**I'm** going to the circus.
9.	**when**	**When** will we go?
10.	**from**	I come **from** Atlanta.

Baby Otter Grows Up
Foal

1. **grow** — Grass can **grow** quickly.
2. **float** — This soap can **float** in water.
3. **show** — **Show** me how this toy works.
4. **growing** — I am **growing** every day.
5. **floating** — Boats were **floating** on the water.
6. **showing** — The dog is **showing** its teeth.
7. **coat** — I wear a **coat** when it's cold.
8. **yellow** — A duckling is **yellow**.
9. **around** — We walked **around** the tree.
10. **old** — My granddad is **old**.

What a Sight!
Lost in the Museum

1. **lie** — **Lie** down and go to sleep.
2. **pie** — I like apple **pie**.
3. **tie** — Can you **tie** your shoes?
4. **night** — At **night** the sky is dark.
5. **light** — Turn on a **light** to see.
6. **right** — Hold up your **right** hand.
7. **cat's** — The **cat's** fur is soft.
8. **dog's** — The **dog's** bark is loud.
9. **been** — Have you **been** to the circus?
10. **found** — I **found** the lost shoe.

254

Chompy's Afternoon
Dinosaur Babies

1. **baby**   A **baby** can crawl.
2. **funny**   The clown was **funny**.
3. **many**   I have **many** friends.
4. **my**   Bill is **my** brother.
5. **why**   **Why** do you smile?
6. **fly**   Birds can **fly**.
7. **without**   I left **without** my raincoat.
8. **nobody**   **Nobody** was at home.
9. **even**   Draw an **even** line for the chart.
10. **most**   That was the **most** fun I ever had.

The True Story of Abbie Burgess
The Bravest Cat! The True Story of Scarlett

1. **new**   I have a **new** baby sister.
2. **grew**   Mom **grew** tomatoes.
3. **drew**   We **drew** pretty pictures.
4. **blue**   Why is the sky **blue**?
5. **true**   This story is **true**.
6. **glue**   Can you **glue** the broken toy?
7. **fixes**   He **fixes** old cars.
8. **washes**   Dad **washes** the dirty dishes.
9. **give**   I will **give** you a gift.
10. **put**   **Put** your coat in the room.

Tested
Word List

A Real Gift
Arthur's Reading Race

buy
only
or
right
think

A Big Day for Jay
Lost!

don't
from
hear
live
when

Baby Otter Grows Up
Foal

around
her
new
old
show

What a Sight!
Lost in the Museum

been
first
found
start
together

Chompy's Afternoon
Dinosaur Babies

animals
even
heard
most
their

The True Story of
Abbie Burgess
The Bravest Cat! The
True Story of Scarlett

because
better
burns
give
people
put

Acknowledgments

Text
Dorling Kindersley (DK) is an international publishing company specializing in the creation of high quality reference content for books, CD-ROMs, online, and video. The hallmark of DK content is its unique combination of educational value and strong visual style—this combination allows DK to deliver appealing, accessible, and engaging educational content that delights children, parents, and teachers around the world. Scott Foresman is delighted to have been able to use selected extracts of DK content within the Scott Foresman Reading program. Page 94: *Foal* by Mary Ling, photographed by Gordon Clayton, pp. 6–21. Copyright © 1992 by Dorling Kindersley Limited.

Page 18: *Arthur's Reading Race* by Marc Brown, pp. 2–23. Text and illustrations copyright © 1996 by Marc Brown. Reprinted by permission of Random House, Inc. Permission granted by Sunny Macmillan for Marc Brown and for Laurie Krasny Brown.
Page 54: *Lost!* by David McPhail. Copyright © 1990 by David McPhail. Reprinted by permission of Little, Brown and Company.
Page 110: "Everything Grows" Words by Raffi, D. Pike. Music by Raffi. © 1987 Homeland Publishing (CAPAC). A division of Troubadour Records Ltd. All rights reserved. Used by permission.
Page 124: *Lost in the Museum* by Miriam Cohen, pictures by Lillian Hoban. Text copyright © 1980 by Miriam Cohen. Used by permission of HarperCollins Publishers.
Page 164: *Dinosaur Babies* by Lucille Recht Penner, illustrated by Peter Barrett. Text copyright © 1991 by Lucille Recht Penner.

Illustrations copyright © 1991 by Peter Barrett. Reprinted by permission of Random House, Inc.
Page 186: "Something Big Has Been Here" from *Something Big Has Been Here* poems by Jack Prelutsky, p. 7. Text copyright © 1990 by Jack Prelutsky. Used by permission of HarperCollins Publishers.
Page 187: "Unfortunately" by Bobbi Katz. Copyright © 1976. Renewed 1995. Reprinted with permission of the poet.
Page 200: Abridgment of *The Bravest Cat!* by Laura Driscoll; illustrated by Dyanne DiSalvo-Ryan. Text copyright © Laura Driscoll, 1997. Illustrations copyright © Dyanne DiSalvo-Ryan, 1997. Published by arrangement with Grosset & Dunlap, an imprint of Penguin Putnam Books for Young Readers, a division of Penguin Putnam Inc.
Page 222: "Kittens" from *Worlds I Know and Other Poems* by Myra Cohn Livingston, p. 8. Reprinted with the permission of Margaret K. McElderry Books, an imprint of Simon & Schuster Children's Publishing Division from *Worlds I Know and Other Poems* by Myra Cohn Livingston. Copyright © 1985 Myra Cohn Livingston.
Selected text and images in this book are copyrighted © 2002.

Artists
Cover illustration © Maryjane Begin; Marc Brown, 18–41; Benrei Huang, 42–45; Lily Hong Hatch, 46–53; David McPhail, 4–5, 54–81, 253; Craig Brown, 82–85; Anna Vojtech, 86–93; Jack Wallen, 110; Ana Maria Guadalupe Ochoa, 112–115; Darryl Ligasan, 116–123; Lillian Hoban, 124–149; Walter Stuart, 150; Jo Ann Adinolfi, 152–155; G. Brian Karas, 6–7, 156–163, 255; Peter

Barrett, 164–185; Claudia Sargent, (border) 164–165; Allan Eitzen, 186, 187; Randy Chewning, 188–189; Pamela Johnson, 190–191; Lane DuPont, 192–199; Fred Willingham, 200–219; Stephanie Britt, 222–223; Robert Alley, 224–227; Don Sullivan, 228; Franklin Hammond, 230–231

Photographs
Every effort has been made to secure permission and provide appropriate credit for photographic material. The publisher deeply regrets any omission and pledges to correct, in subsequent editions, errors called to its attention.
Unless otherwise acknowledged, all photographs are the property of Scott Foresman, a division of Pearson Education. Page abbreviations are as follows: (t) top, (b) bottom, (l) left, (r) right, (ins) inset, (s) spot, (bk) background.
Page 41 Susan Cohen (TL) Courtesy Marc Brown; Page 81 Richard Hutchings (CL) Richard Hutchings; Page 86 (C) Alan D. Carey/Photo Researchers, Inc.; Page 93 (C) © Walter Chandoha; Page 110 photo copyright © by Bruce McMillan; Page 111 (BL) photo copyright © by Bruce McMillan; Page 111 (C) photo copyright © by Bruce McMillan; Page 111 (TR) photo copyright © by Bruce McMillan; Page 151 William Morrow (BL) Courtesy, William Morrow; Page 151 Miriam Cohen (TL) Courtesy Miriam Cohen; Page 220 (TC) AP/Wide World

Glossary
The contents of this glossary have been adapted from *My First Dictionary*. Copyright © 2000 by Scott, Foresman and Company, a division of Addison Wesley Educational Publishers, Inc.